THE PROMISES OF GOD HANDBOOK

A Journey Into His faithfulness

Alisa L. Grace

Self-Published by
Alisa L. Grace
Sanford, FL 32771
sirrenderedforlife.com

ISBN: 978-1-966129-78-3

First Edition

Printed in the United States of America

Library of Congress Cataloging-in-Publication Data
Grace, Alisa L.
Title of the Book: The Promises of God Handbook: A Journey Into His faithfulness

Acknowledgments: The author wishes to thank God, Her Husband (Linion), Victory Temple of God, Florida SPECS, Unity Youth Association, All About Serving You, Angels-ANJ Events, NordeVest, and Love & Create Life for their support and contributions.

TABLE OF CONTENTS

INTRODUCTION:

LIVING BY THE PROMISES OF GOD

God's promises are the lifeline of the believer. They are not just hopeful thoughts or kind encouragements — they are declarations of what God *will* do, anchored in His unchanging nature and perfect faithfulness. The purpose of this handbook is to help believers understand, believe, and stand on the promises of God in every season of life.

The Word of God says in **2 Corinthians 1:20**, *"For all the promises of God in Him are Yes, and in Him Amen, to the glory of God through us."* This means every promise made by God is affirmed and fulfilled in Jesus Christ. When we align our lives with His Word and will, we can confidently hold on to these promises no matter what we face.

Each section of this handbook is categorized by life situations — from daily needs to spiritual growth, trials, and eternal hope — with corresponding scriptures and reflections to guide you. Use this handbook in your quiet time, for Scripture memorization, or to pray over your circumstances with bold faith.

Purpose of the Handbook

The purpose of this handbook is to *strengthen your faith by anchoring your heart in the unshakable promises of God*. In a world that is constantly changing — filled with uncertainty, anxiety, trials, and spiritual battles — God's promises offer stability, clarity, and power. His Word is not only a source of truth but also a foundation on which we can confidently build our lives.

This handbook is a spiritual resource for believers of all ages and walks of life. Whether you're new to the faith or have been walking with the Lord for decades, this guide is designed to help you:

- **Discover what God has said and still says** to His people today.

- **Declare those promises aloud** to align your words with God's truth.

- **Dwell in His presence** by meditating on the Scriptures.

- **Develop unwavering trust** through consistent exposure to His faithfulness.

This is more than a collection of encouraging verses — it is a manual for victorious living. When you learn to stand on what God has promised, you are no longer a victim of your circumstances; you become a victor through Christ who lives in you.

How to Use the Handbook for Daily Encouragement, Prayer, and Study

---

This handbook is designed to be *interactive and life-giving*, not just read but lived. Here are a few practical ways to integrate it into your daily rhythm:

1. Daily Encouragement

Each section contains categorized promises that you can refer to according to your need for the day. Are you feeling anxious? Go to the "Peace" or "Protection" section. Are you discouraged? Turn to "Strength" or "Victory in Trials." Speak the promises aloud. Let them become your *first response*, not your last resort.

2. Prayer Tool

Use the promises as a foundation for powerful, faith-filled prayers. Pray the Word back to God by inserting your name or situation into the verse. For example:

"Lord, Your Word says You will supply all my needs (Philippians 4:19). Today, I trust You to provide for my rent, my family, and my future. You are my Shepherd; I shall not want."

You can also create prayer declarations and confession cards based on each promise.

3. Bible Study Companion

Take time to meditate on each verse. Read the surrounding chapter for deeper understanding. Use journaling prompts to reflect on:

- What is God revealing to me through this promise?

- How does this apply to my current life season?

- What action step is the Holy Spirit leading me to take?

You may choose one category per week or focus on one promise per day, using this as a month-long devotional.

Pair it with worship music and quiet time for deeper connection.

A Reminder That All God's Promises Are "Yes and Amen" in Christ (2 Corinthians 1:20)

"For all the promises of God in Him are Yes, and in Him Amen, to the glory of God through us." – 2 Corinthians 1:20 (NKJV)

This powerful verse is the cornerstone of the entire handbook. It means that every single promise God made in Scripture — whether for provision, peace, strength, healing, salvation, or guidance — finds its *fulfillment in Jesus Christ*. Jesus is the "Yes" — the divine confirmation that God's Word is true and will be accomplished. The "Amen" is our agreement and faith-filled response: *So be it, Lord!*

When you see a promise in the Bible, you don't have to wonder if it applies to you. If you are in Christ, that promise is yours. Jesus has already secured it through His finished work on the cross. God's promises are not based on how good we are, but on how good Jesus is. We receive them by grace through faith.

This reminder is essential because it shifts our mindset from *doubt* to *certainty*, from *striving* to *trusting*. As you walk through each section of this handbook, let this verse echo in your heart: *"If God promised it, then Jesus has made it possible for me to receive it."*

PART 1:

PROMISES FOR DAILY LIFE

Introduction

God cares about your everyday needs — not just your spiritual growth but your practical, emotional, and physical well-being. He wants you to experience peace, provision, protection, and strength day by day. In this section, you will discover promises that remind you that you are never alone in your daily journey.

---

1. Provision

"I see what you need before you even ask." – Jesus

You wake up with worry in your heart. Bills, responsibilities, and a long to-do list cloud your peace. You sit quietly, unsure how the day will unfold. Then, in the stillness, you hear Him — not audibly, but within.

"Beloved, why are you anxious? I am your Shepherd. I care for the birds of the air and clothe the lilies of the field — how much more will I provide for you? I am not blind to your needs. I know every detail of your life, and I have already made a way. My provision isn't limited by what you see. My supply flows from Heaven's storehouses, not earth's systems."

Philippians 4:19 – "And my God will supply all your needs according to His riches in glory in Christ Jesus."

This promise assures you that God's provision is not based on earthly limitations but on His eternal riches. Whether you're facing financial lack, emotional emptiness, or spiritual hunger, God is your ultimate Source.

Psalm 23:1 – "The Lord is my shepherd; I shall not want."

As your Good Shepherd, God takes personal responsibility for your care. This promise speaks of ongoing provision — you will not lack what you truly need, because He is watching over you.

He continues,

"Provision isn't about riches. It's about trust. Look back and see: Have I ever left you without? Even in the waiting, I was working. Trust Me again today."

🌀 Transformative Questions:

1. Where in your life do you struggle to trust that God will provide?

2. Can you recall a time God met your need in an unexpected way?

🙏 Prayer Prompt:

Jesus, help me rest in the truth that You are my Shepherd. I surrender every anxious thought and every need. Teach me to look to You as my Source and not the world. Provide for me in the way You know is best, and help me recognize Your hand when it comes.

---

2. Protection

"I am your refuge — run into My arms." – Jesus

You feel the pressures mounting — threats of failure, fears about your children, concerns about your safety. You look around for someone to shield you, and Jesus draws near.

"My child, you are not exposed — you are covered. I am your fortress, your hiding place. Come dwell in the secret place with Me, and no harm will overtake you. Even when the enemy forms weapons against you, they will not prosper."

Psalm 91:1-4 – "He who dwells in the shelter of the Most High will rest in the shadow of the Almighty..."

This passage is a powerful shield for the believer. It promises protection from danger, fear, and harm for those who stay close to God. When you abide in Him, you are spiritually and even physically covered by His divine care.

Isaiah 54:17 – "No weapon formed against you shall prosper..."

This is a promise of spiritual security. Even when you are attacked by circumstances, people, or the enemy himself, nothing that is formed against you will succeed. God is your defender.

"You're not fighting alone," He assures you.

"I've already won the battle. Your job is to rest, trust, and stay close."

You exhale. He's fighting for you.

🔄 Transformative Questions:

1. What fears or threats have made you forget that God is your Protector?

2. How would your decisions change if you truly believed you were divinely covered?

🔒 Prayer Prompt:

Jesus, thank You for being my Protector. Even when I don't see the danger, You do — and You cover me. Strengthen my trust in Your divine defense. Hide me in Your shadow and teach me to run to You, not from You, in times of fear.

---

3. Peace

"I give you peace the world can't take away."
– Jesus

Your mind races. There's tension in your chest, knots in your stomach, and no amount of distractions ease the unrest. You whisper, "Lord, I need peace." And He's already there.

"Peace isn't the absence of trouble — it's My Presence in the midst of it. I don't give as the world gives. My peace is deep, still, and powerful. Let Me speak to your storm."

John 14:27 – "Peace I leave with you; My peace I give to you..."

Jesus offers a peace that the world cannot give. This promise is for your heart and mind in a chaotic world. His peace is a supernatural calmness, even in the middle of storms.

Isaiah 26:3 – "You will keep him in perfect peace whose mind is stayed on You..."

Peace is the fruit of focus. This promise teaches that when we fix our thoughts on God and trust Him, He guards our hearts with a peace that surpasses understanding.

"Keep your thoughts on Me," He says gently.

"Don't be pulled away by what-ifs and maybes. I am here, and I am enough. My peace guards hearts and minds."

The noise in your head fades. His voice anchors you.

⊙ Transformative Questions:

1. What thoughts or distractions are robbing you of peace today?

2. What would happen if you redirected your mind to Jesus in every anxious moment?

🙏 Prayer Prompt:

Jesus, I receive Your peace. Not the kind the world offers — temporary and hollow — but Your deep, abiding peace. Quiet the noise inside me. Let my thoughts be rooted in You. Thank You for being the calm in my chaos.

---

4. Strength

"When you are weak, I am strong in you."
– Jesus

You feel exhausted — physically, emotionally, spiritually. You whisper, "I can't do this." And Jesus replies, "That's exactly where I step in."

"Your strength was never meant to carry you through. Mine is perfect in your weakness. When you reach the end of yourself, you find the beginning of My power."

Isaiah 40:31 – "But they that wait upon the Lord shall renew their strength…"

This promise assures you that waiting on God is not passive — it is active trust. As you hope in Him, He revives your strength, lifting you above weariness like an eagle on the wind.

2 Corinthians 12:9 – "My grace is sufficient for you, for My power is made perfect in weakness."

God doesn't remove all weaknesses; instead, He fills your weakness with His power. This promise reminds you that in your lowest moments, His strength is greatest.

"Let Me be your strength," He whispers.

"I won't just help you crawl — I'll help you soar. Don't despise your limitations. In them, I do My greatest work."

Your weakness becomes a doorway. His strength becomes your banner.

⚙ Transformative Questions:

1. Where have you been trying to carry something in your own strength?

2. What would it look like to embrace your weakness as a place of divine power?

🛐 Prayer Prompt:

Jesus, I confess my weakness — not with shame, but with surrender. I need Your strength. Help me wait on You, trust in You, and receive Your grace daily. Be my endurance when I'm tired, my resolve when I want to quit, and my power when I feel empty.

PART 2:

PROMISES FOR SPIRITUAL GROWTH

Jesus Speaks Life into Your Soul

Introduction

You were made for Me.

Before you ever took a breath, I formed you with a purpose — not just to exist, but to *walk with Me*. Deep down, you've felt it. That ache, that longing, that quiet emptiness that no success, relationship, achievement, or distraction has ever truly filled.

That's because it wasn't meant to be filled with anything but Me.

I am not just a Sunday sermon. I'm not a distant deity watching from afar. I am your *Father*. Your *Friend*. Your *Redeemer*. And I miss you.

You see, spiritual growth isn't about performing for Me. It's about *knowing Me*. Let Me say that again, slowly — *It's about knowing Me*. Talking with Me. Walking with Me. Trusting Me. Letting Me speak into the deepest places of your heart. I created you for relationship, not religion. That's the missing piece. That's what your soul has been craving.

This section is an invitation to come closer — not in shame, but in love. Not out of duty, but out of desire. These promises are not just Scriptures to memorize; they are *truths to live from*, gifts from My heart to yours. As you read, let go of the noise, the pretending, the striving. Just come sit with Me. I want to walk with you, grow with you, and transform your life from the inside out.

---

5. Guidance

"I will show you the way — I always have. You've just been trying to navigate life without Me." – Jesus

You've been trying so hard to figure things out — to make the right decisions, build the right life, avoid the wrong turns. But every time you try to carry it on your own, you feel the weight of confusion and fear. You whisper, "God, I just don't know what to do anymore." And I hear you.

"My precious one, when did you start believing that you had to figure it all out without Me? I've been here, all along — waiting to lead you. If you'll trust Me, I'll take you step by step, even when you can't see the whole road ahead. I don't expect you to have it all together. I just want you to walk with Me."

Proverbs 3:5–6 – "Trust in the Lord with all your heart... and He shall direct your paths."

Life presents many choices, and this promise is your compass. When you stop leaning on your understanding and start resting in God's love and voice, He leads you with precision and peace.

Psalm 32:8 – "I will instruct you and teach you in the way you should go..."

God is not distant or silent. He is a personal Guide, eager to walk beside you and illuminate the path when you invite Him in.

"Your confusion doesn't scare Me," I say gently.

"But your independence keeps you wandering. Come closer. Let Me lead."

🌀 **Transformative Questions:**

1. Have you been walking through life trying to guide yourself without Jesus?

2. What decisions would feel lighter if you trusted Him to lead instead of leaning on yourself?

🙏 **Prayer Prompt:**

Jesus, I've been trying to lead my own life, and I'm tired. I don't want to do this without You anymore. Guide me. Whisper Your direction into my spirit. I want to walk with You — not just ask You to bless my way. Teach me to trust Your voice.

---

6. Wisdom

"You've been listening to everyone but Me. But I'm the only One who sees it all — and I want to share My heart with you." – Jesus

You scroll for answers. You search YouTube, books, podcasts, and people for advice. You've heard so many voices that you don't know who to believe anymore. But one voice has been waiting, patiently, to be heard.

"Beloved, I am the Source of wisdom — not just for big life questions, but for every part of your life: how you speak, love, rest, parent, serve, and dream. You don't need a perfect plan — you need *My perspective*. When you ask Me, I give you more than answers — I give you *understanding*. I give you *clarity*. I give you *truth that sets you free*."

> **James 1:5 – "If any of you lacks wisdom, let him ask of God... and it will be given to him."**

You don't need to qualify for God's wisdom — just ask in faith. He's not holding back. He wants to pour it into every area of your life.

> **Proverbs 2:6 – "For the Lord gives wisdom; from His mouth come knowledge and understanding."**

Wisdom flows from intimacy with God. It comes from knowing His Word and hearing His heart.

"Stop settling for opinions," I whisper.

"Come sit with Me. Let Me teach you how to live free and full."

🌀 **Transformative Questions:**

1.   Where have you been seeking wisdom apart from your relationship with Jesus?

2.   What if the wisdom you need is found in the time you spend in His presence?

🙏 **Prayer Prompt:**

Jesus, I need Your wisdom — not the world's opinions, but Your truth. Open my heart to hear You clearly. Help me slow down, turn off the noise, and lean into Your Word. Speak wisdom over every part of my life — I will listen and follow.

---

7. Forgiveness & Cleansing

"You don't have to hide anymore. I already knew, and I still want you." – Jesus

There's something you've been carrying — a weight, a regret, a hidden shame. You've tried to bury it under busyness or disguise it with a smile. But inside, you wonder: "Would God really love me if He knew?"

"I do know," I say, kneeling beside your brokenness.

"And I love you. I always have. I'm not shocked by your sin — I carried it. I took the punishment, the guilt, the shame. I went to the cross so you wouldn't have to hide in fear or carry this alone. Come. Let Me wash you clean. Not just forgive — *cleanse*. I want to make you whole again."

1 John 1:9 – "If we confess our sins, He is faithful and just to forgive us…"

Confession isn't about shame — it's about restoration. When you bring your sin into the light, Jesus covers it with His grace and makes you new.

Isaiah 1:18 – "Though your sins are like scarlet, they shall be as white as snow…"

God's forgiveness is not temporary or partial. He makes you brand new — your past does not define your future.

"You are not your failure," I whisper.

"You are Mine. And I will never turn away from a heart that returns to Me."

🌀 Transformative Questions:

1. What burden of guilt or shame have you been carrying that Jesus is ready to lift?

2. What would it look like to walk in the freedom of full forgiveness?

🙏 Prayer Prompt:

Jesus, I'm done hiding. I bring You everything — the sin, the secrets, the stains. Thank You for seeing it all and still loving me. Wash me clean. Heal my heart. Teach me how to live forgiven and free. I want to walk in intimacy with You again.

PART 3:

PROMISES FOR DIFFICULT TIMES

Jesus Walks With You Through the Fire

Introduction

You don't have to pretend with Me.

You may be smiling on the outside, but I see the storm within — the ache you can't explain, the weight no one else seems to notice, the tears you cry alone in the dark. I see it *all*. And I'm not repelled by your pain — I'm drawn to it.

You were never meant to carry heartbreak, fear, or confusion alone. I'm the only One who truly understands how to walk you through it — because I've been there. I was misunderstood, betrayed, mocked, abandoned, and even crucified. I know the depths of suffering, and I promise you this: I will not let your pain be wasted.

The world tells you to "be strong," but I tell you to "come to Me." Let Me hold you. Let Me carry you. Let Me walk you through the fire — not around it, but *through it*, safely, so you come out changed but never consumed. These promises are not clichés or feel-good sayings. They are *anchors for your soul* when the waters rise.

Let My words become your lifeline. Let My presence become your peace.

---

8. Comfort in Sorrow

"I see your tears... and I catch every one."
– Jesus

You didn't ask for this. You didn't see it coming. And now you feel like you're walking through life in pieces — holding on, but barely. Others may not know how deeply you're hurting, but I do. You've been whispering, "Why, Lord?" and "Where are You?"

"I'm right here," I whisper.

"Closer than your breath. Nearer than your pain. I'm not a distant God watching from a safe distance — I draw close to the brokenhearted. When you ache, I'm aching too. I don't rush your healing; I stay with you in it. I comfort. I carry. I restore."

Psalm 34:18 – "The Lord is close to the brokenhearted and saves those who are crushed in spirit."

This is not just poetic — it's personal. When your heart breaks, God moves in even closer. He is a Savior not only from sin but from sorrow.

2 Corinthians 1:3–4 – "The God of all comfort... comforts us in all our troubles..."

God doesn't only comfort us for our sake — He equips us through our pain to become comforters for others. No tear is wasted.

"I collect your tears," I whisper.

"I remember every cry. And I promise, joy will come again. But for now, just let Me hold you."

🌀 Transformative Questions:

1. What hidden grief have you been carrying alone that Jesus is ready to comfort?

2. How have you seen God's presence show up even in your pain?

🙏 Prayer Prompt:

Jesus, I need You in my sorrow. I don't have words — just tears. Thank You for being near when I feel broken. Wrap me in Your arms, hold my shattered heart, and remind me that I'm not alone. Be my Comforter today and always.

---

9. Deliverance from Fear

"You don't have to live afraid — I am with you."
– Jesus

Fear has crept into your thoughts like a shadow — fear of the future, fear of failure, fear of losing control. You've tried to ignore it, suppress it, or outrun it, but it lingers. And when the night comes and the distractions fade, it speaks loudest.

But then I lean in.

"Child, fear is a liar. And it doesn't come from Me. I gave you *power*, not panic. *Love*, not torment. *Peace*, not dread. Fear has been robbing you of joy, sleep, and clarity — but today, you can take it back. Not because you're fearless, but because I'm with you."

2 Timothy 1:7 – "For God has not given us a spirit of fear, but of power and of love and of a sound mind."

Fear is not from God. He has replaced fear with identity — you are powerful, deeply loved, and capable of sound thinking through the Spirit.

Psalm 34:4 – "I sought the Lord, and He answered me; He delivered me from all my fears."

This is not a partial deliverance — it's complete. The fear that haunts you is no match for the presence of the Lord.

"Stop trying to fight fear on your own," I whisper.

"Invite Me in. Let My love push fear out. I promise — you're safe with Me."

☉ Transformative Questions:

1. What fear has been holding you hostage that Jesus wants to deliver you from?

2. What would life look like if you truly believed you are safe in God's love?

🔒 Prayer Prompt:

Jesus, fear has been louder than faith in some areas of my life. But today, I run into Your arms. I reject the spirit of fear and receive Your peace, love, and power. Help me stand in truth when lies try to speak. I trust that You are with me.

---

10. Victory in Trials

"This won't break you — it will build you."
– Jesus

You're in the middle of a storm. It's confusing, stretching, painful, and it feels never-ending. You wonder, "How can anything good come from this?" You've prayed. You've believed. But you're still in the thick of it. Then I draw near.

"You don't see the whole story yet — but I do. You see pressure, I see preparation. You feel pain, I see purpose.

Every trial is not an ending — it's a doorway. Through it, I'm refining you. Strengthening you. Maturing you. *Don't quit in the middle.* Victory is ahead."

Romans 8:28 – "And we know that all things work together for good to those who love God..."

This promise doesn't say all things *are* good, but that God works *through* all things to bring about something good — something eternal and life-shaping.

James 1:12 – "Blessed is the one who perseveres under trial..."

God honors the one who holds on. Trials will come, but so will the reward — deeper faith, tested endurance, and crowns of glory.

"The trial will end," I whisper,

"But the treasure I'm producing in you will last forever."

🌀 Transformative Questions:

1. How have you been viewing your current trial — as a punishment or a preparation?

2. What is Jesus refining in you during this difficult season?

🛐 Prayer Prompt:

Jesus, I don't understand everything I'm walking through — but I know You're with me. Give me eyes to see the purpose in my pain. Give me the endurance to hold on. I choose to believe that this trial will not define me — it will develop me. Let Your victory be my strength.

PART 4:

PROMISES FOR FUTURE HOPE

Jesus Is the Hope That Never Fails

Introduction

There's something inside you — something quiet, maybe almost hidden — that wonders, *Is everything going to be okay?*

That ache for security... that longing for something more... that whisper that says *this world can't be all there is* — it's not random. It's Me.

I put eternity in your heart.

You were never meant to feel at home in a broken world. That's why, no matter how much you achieve, collect, or experience, something always feels just out of reach. You were made for *My presence*, for *My Kingdom*, for *a forever that cannot be shaken*.

And here's the truth I want to plant deep in your soul:

I have never broken a promise — and I never will.

What I said I will do, I *will* do. The future is not uncertain when it's in My hands. When the world grows darker, My light shines brighter. When headlines scream chaos, My Word whispers truth. When your heart feels restless, I become your peace.

Every promise I've made about your future — your eternal life, My return, your restoration, your reward — is sealed in My blood and guaranteed by My faithfulness.

Let Me remind you of what's coming. Let Me anchor you in hope. You are not drifting — you are *held*.

---

11. Eternal Life

"Forever with Me — this is your destiny."
– Jesus

This life has brought joy, yes... but it's also brought heartbreak, disappointment, and grief. You've stood beside graves. You've watched dreams die. You've wondered why good things end. And in quiet moments, you ask, "What happens after this?"

Then I answer:

"Child, this life is not the end — it's the beginning. The moment you gave Me your heart, you stepped into eternity. Eternal life is not just about someday — it's about *now*. It's the deep knowing that no matter what happens here, *you are Mine forever*. I've prepared a place for you. I've written your name in My Book. You don't have to fear death — because I already conquered it."

John 3:16 – "For God so loved the world, that He gave His only begotten Son, that whoever believes in Him shall not perish but have eternal life."

This is the foundation of your faith. God's love purchased eternal life for you — not based on your performance, but on His Son's sacrifice.

1 John 2:25 – "This is the promise that He has promised us — eternal life."

God's promise is not vague or uncertain. It's clear, assured, and sealed. If He promised eternal life, you *have* it. You can live with confidence and peace.

"Every tear will be wiped away," I whisper.

"Every wound will be healed. And you will see Me face to face."

🌀 Transformative Questions:

1. Do you truly live with the confidence that eternal life is already yours?

2. How would your choices and peace change if you remembered daily that death is not the end?

🙏 Prayer Prompt:

Jesus, thank You for the promise of eternal life. Sometimes I forget that this world is not my home. Help me to live each day with my heart rooted in Heaven. Fill me with peace, knowing that no matter what I face, my eternity is secure in You.

12. Jesus' Return

"I'm coming back — and I haven't forgotten you." – Jesus

Sometimes, the world feels like it's spinning out of control. Evil seems louder. Darkness seems stronger. And you ask, "Jesus, when are You coming back?" It's not a question of doubt — it's a cry of longing. And I hear it.

"I have not forgotten you. I have not changed My mind. I will return — just as I said. Not as a quiet carpenter, but as the King of Glory. The skies will split. Every knee will bow. Every injustice will be exposed. And I will wipe away every tear. I'm not slow in keeping My promise — I'm patient, waiting so more hearts can be saved. But make no mistake: *I am coming back for you.*"

John 14:2–3 – "I go to prepare a place for you... I will come again and receive you to Myself; that where I am, there you may be also."

Jesus didn't just leave — He left with a plan. He is actively preparing a place for you, and His return is guaranteed. It's not a matter of *if*, but *when*.

Revelation 22:12 – "Behold, I am coming soon. My reward is with Me..."

Jesus is not coming empty-handed — He's coming with reward, with restoration, with righteousness. He's coming as the fulfillment of every longing.

"Keep watching," I whisper.

"Not with fear, but with *hope*. You were made for My return."

🌀 Transformative Questions:

1. How often do you meditate on and prepare your heart for the return of Jesus?

2. What in your life today would change if you lived with urgency and expectancy for His return?

🙏 Prayer Prompt:

Jesus, thank You for Your promise to return. Forgive me for growing too comfortable in a world that is not my home. Stir my heart with holy longing. Teach me to live alert, awake, and anchored in the hope that You are coming back — for me.

Final Word:

A LOVE LETTER FROM JESUS TO YOU

My Child, My Promise Still Stands

You've walked with Me through the pages of this book — page by page, word by word. You've heard My voice. You've felt My presence. You've learned My promises.

And now, I want you to pause — and breathe.

Because I'm not finished speaking. I want to look you in the eyes and remind you:

I am the same yesterday, today, and forever.
I do not change. I do not forget. I do not fail.

Everything I've said to you — from the very beginning — I will fulfill.

You've read how I provide.

You've read how I protect.

You've read how I give peace, how I strengthen you, guide you, give wisdom, forgive you, comfort you, deliver you, sustain you in trials, and promise you eternal life.

You've read that I'm coming back for you.

And none of it — not a single promise — is too good to be true. Because **I AM Truth.**

My promises are not based on your perfection, but on My character. They are not earned — they are received. They are not empty words — they are *covenant words*, sealed in My blood.

Even when you've doubted Me, I remained faithful.

Even when you've wandered, I never walked away.

Even when you couldn't trace My hand, My heart was still working for you — behind the scenes, ahead of the scenes, and right beside you.

The enemy will try to steal My promises from your heart. He'll whisper lies:

"God forgot you. You're too far gone. It's too late. Maybe it wasn't for you."

But let Me silence those lies once and for all:

I never forget. I never change My mind. And you are never too far gone for My grace.

I am your Shepherd, your Shield, your Anchor, your Father, your Friend, and your soon-coming King.

Everything I've promised, I *will* perform.

So walk forward now — not in fear, but in *faith*.

Not in shame, but in *confidence*.

Not in striving, but in *surrender*.

Keep this book close, but keep My Word even closer.

When life shakes you, *stand on what I said*.

When the world lets you down, *lean into My faithfulness*.

When your heart grows tired, *run back into My arms*.

I will always be waiting.

And My promises will still be true.

I love you — always and forever.

I am the Promise Keeper.

And I will never fail you.

– Jesus

PERSONAL COMMITMENT LETTER FROM THE READER TO GOD

My Response to You, Lord

Jesus,

As I close this book, I open my heart wider than ever before.

I hear You. I feel You. I believe You.

You are not just a distant God — You are my Father, my Friend, my Savior, and my Sustainer.

I acknowledge today that **You are the missing piece** I've been searching for.

No more running. No more wandering.

I choose You — not just as my belief, but as my *relationship*.

I choose to live by Your promises — to hold onto them, walk in them, speak them, and trust them.

Where I've doubted, I now believe.

Where I've feared, I now trust.

Where I've strayed, I now return.

Where I've been weak, I now lean on Your strength.

From this day forward, I commit to walk in relationship with You — not out of duty, but from a place of love and faith.

I will make Your Word my foundation, Your promises my daily bread, and Your presence my home.

You are my **Sure Thing**, Jesus.

And I will never stop believing in You.

With all my heart,

I make this commitment — not just with my pen, but with my life.

Signed: _____

Date: _____

APPENDIX

How to Declare God's Promises Daily

Living from Victory, Not for It

Declaring God's promises is not wishful thinking — it's *faith-filled alignment*. When you declare His Word over your life, you're not trying to convince God to move — you're agreeing with what He has already said. Declarations invite His truth into your thoughts, emotions, circumstances, and atmosphere.

Here's how to do it with intentionality:

🛠 1. Choose a Promise Based on Your Need

Are you feeling anxious? Declare a promise of peace.

Facing a financial need? Declare a promise of provision.

Battling fear? Declare God's protection and power.

Let your need lead you to the truth — and then let truth reshape the way you think and speak.

🗣 2. Speak the Word Out Loud — Daily

The power of life and death is in the tongue (Proverbs 18:21). When you speak God's promises aloud, they rewire your faith and shift the atmosphere. Don't just think it — say it. Speak it with authority, knowing His Word does not return void (Isaiah 55:11).

Example:

"God, You are my Shepherd. I will not lack today. You will supply all my needs. I trust You. I am not alone, and I will not be afraid."

3. Personalize the Promise

Insert your name, your situation, and your language. Don't recite — *relate*. You're not quoting Scripture as a robot; you're engaging with your Father as a child.

Example:

"Jesus, Your Word says You give peace — not like the world. I receive that peace right now in my body, my mind, and my heart. My name is written on Your hand, and I am safe in You."

🔁 4. Repeat it Until You Believe it

Sometimes it takes repetition to break strongholds of fear, doubt, or shame. That's okay. Keep declaring it until your heart aligns with your mouth. Faith comes by hearing (Romans 10:17) — even when the one speaking is *you*.

30-Day Promise Declaration Challenge

Speak Life. See Change.

This challenge is designed to help you **build a habit of speaking God's promises every day**. Each day includes a declaration category and a sample verse to declare aloud. You can write it down, speak it out loud, or post it somewhere visible — just make sure it enters your heart through repetition and faith.

Week 1: Provision & Peace

1. God provides all my needs. *(Philippians 4:19)*

2. The Lord is my Shepherd. I lack nothing. *(Psalm 23:1)*

3. I trust God to give me daily bread. *(Matthew 6:11)*

4. Jesus is my peace in every storm. *(John 14:27)*

5. My mind is stayed on God, and I have peace. *(Isaiah 26:3)*

6. I am anxious for nothing; I pray and receive peace. *(Philippians 4:6–7)*

7. I walk in perfect peace because God is with me.

Week 2: Protection & Strength

8. I dwell in the shelter of the Most High. *(Psalm 91:1)*

9. No weapon formed against me shall prosper. *(Isaiah 54:17)*

10. God is my refuge and strength. *(Psalm 46:1)*

11. I am strong in the Lord and in His mighty power. *(Ephesians 6:10)*

12. His grace is sufficient for me. *(2 Corinthians 12:9)*

13. I wait on the Lord, and He renews my strength. *(Isaiah 40:31)*

14. I can do all things through Christ. *(Philippians 4:13)*

Week 3: Wisdom, Guidance & Forgiveness

15. God is directing my path. *(Proverbs 3:5–6)*

16. God is instructing and teaching me. *(Psalm 32:8)*

17. I ask and receive wisdom generously. *(James 1:5)*

18. God gives wisdom, understanding, and insight. *(Proverbs 2:6)*

19. I confess my sin, and He forgives and cleanses me. *(1 John 1:9)*

20. Though my sins were scarlet, He made me white as snow. *(Isaiah 1:18)*

21. I walk in the freedom of forgiveness and grace.

Week 4: Comfort, Deliverance, Victory & Hope

22. God is near to my broken heart. *(Psalm 34:18)*

23. He comforts me in all my troubles. *(2 Corinthians 1:3–4)*

24. I am delivered from all my fears. *(Psalm 34:4)*

25. I have not been given a spirit of fear. *(2 Timothy 1:7)*

26. God is working all things for my good. *(Romans 8:28)*

27. I am blessed when I persevere under trial. *(James 1:12)*

28. I have eternal life through Jesus. *(1 John 2:25)*

29. Jesus has gone to prepare a place for me. *(John 14:2–3)*

30. Jesus is coming soon — and I am ready. *(Revelation 22:12)*

Prayer Prompts for Each Promise Category

Turn the Promises into Intimate Conversations

Use these guided prompts to turn God's promises into daily, heartfelt prayers. They are starting points — you can expand them as the Holy Spirit leads.

Provision

"Father, You know every need in my life — physical, emotional, and spiritual. I release my worry and ask You to be my Provider today. Supply what I need in Your timing and in Your way. Help me to trust You even when I cannot see how."

Protection

"Lord, I take refuge in You. Cover me under Your wings. Keep my mind, body, and spirit safe from harm, fear, and temptation. Let Your angels surround my home, my family, and my future. Thank You for being my Defender."

Peace

"Jesus, quiet the noise around and inside me. I invite Your perfect peace into my heart and mind. Remove anxiety and fear, and help me keep my thoughts fixed on You. Thank You that You are the calm in every storm."

Strength

"Holy Spirit, I feel weak — but I know You are strong. Fill me with fresh strength today. Help me rise up like an eagle and keep moving forward in grace. Remind me that Your power is made perfect in my weakness."

Guidance

"God, I need Your direction. I don't want to take another step without You. Teach me, lead me, and show me the way. Close every wrong door and open the right ones. I trust Your timing, Your plan, and Your voice."

Wisdom

"Lord, I ask for wisdom today — not the wisdom of the world, but from Your Spirit. Help me make decisions that honor You. Give me clarity, discernment, and insight. Speak truth to me when I'm uncertain."

Forgiveness

"Jesus, I come to You honestly. You see it all — and yet You love me. I confess my sin and ask for Your forgiveness. Cleanse my heart, heal my wounds, and remind me I am fully forgiven and restored."

Comfort

"Father, I feel the weight of sorrow. Please meet me in this pain. Wrap me in Your arms and breathe peace over me. Thank You for being close to the brokenhearted. I receive Your comfort and healing now."

Deliverance

"Lord, I ask You to deliver me from fear, strongholds, and every lie I've believed. Set me free from anything that doesn't reflect You. I declare that I am not a slave — I am free in Christ. Lead me into liberty."

Victory in Trials

"God, this season has been hard. But I believe You are working even when I can't see it. Strengthen me to endure, mature me through the process, and reveal the purpose in the pain. I trust You for the victory."

Eternal Life & Jesus' Return

"Jesus, thank You for the promise of forever. Remind me daily that this world is not my home. Keep me watchful, hopeful, and ready for Your return. I live today with eternity in mind — because You are coming back for me."

www.ingramcontent.com/pod-product-compliance
Lightning Source LLC
LaVergne TN
LVHW051430080426
835508LV00022B/3325